Rupert McCall is a Queensland-based poet. In 1994, at the age of 24, he left his solicitor's office to pour his passion and energy into the verses emerging from his pen and hasn't looked back. He recites his work regularly at a wide variety of gatherings, from business and corporate functions to sporting occasions and is in great demand on the speakers' circuit. With regular newspaper columns, radio spots and television appearances, his profile is growing daily throughout Australia.

Rupert's collection of poetry has accumulated significantly, a fact highlighted by the publication of two previous anthologies: *Rupert ... Rhymes, Idols and Shenanigans* and the best-seller *Slops, Props and Goosestep Flavoured Lifesavers*.

Rupert's poetry is a colourful expression of verse, inspired by achievements, sporting and otherwise. When his spirit and emotion is triggered, you can bet that poetry will be his means of communication. He is fiercely proud. *Green & Gold Malaria* is a reflection of the love he has for his country, beautifully written and tastefully presented in a style uniquely Rupert's.

For further information on Rupert, contact the following Internet address:

http://www.gmg.com.au/rupert

GREEN & GOLD MALARIA

RUPERT McCALL

Published 1996 by Mandarin
a part of Reed Books Australia
7/35 Cotham Road, Kew, Victoria 3101
a division of Reed International Books Australia Pty Limited
Reprinted 1996 (twice)

Copyright © Rupert McCall 1996

All rights reserved. Without limiting the rights under copyright above, no part of this publication may be reproduced, stored in or introduced into a retrieval system, or transmitted in any form or by any means (electronic, mechanical, photocopying, recording or otherwise), without the prior written permission of both the copyright owner and the publisher.

Illustrated by Scott Rigney
Typeset in New Baskerville and Copperplate by Bookset Type & Image
Printed and bound in Australia by Australian Print Group

National Library of Australia
  cataloguing-in-publication data:

McCall, Rupert.
  Green and gold malaria.

ISBN 1 86330 609 9.

I. Title.

A821.3

To my brothers who travelled with me

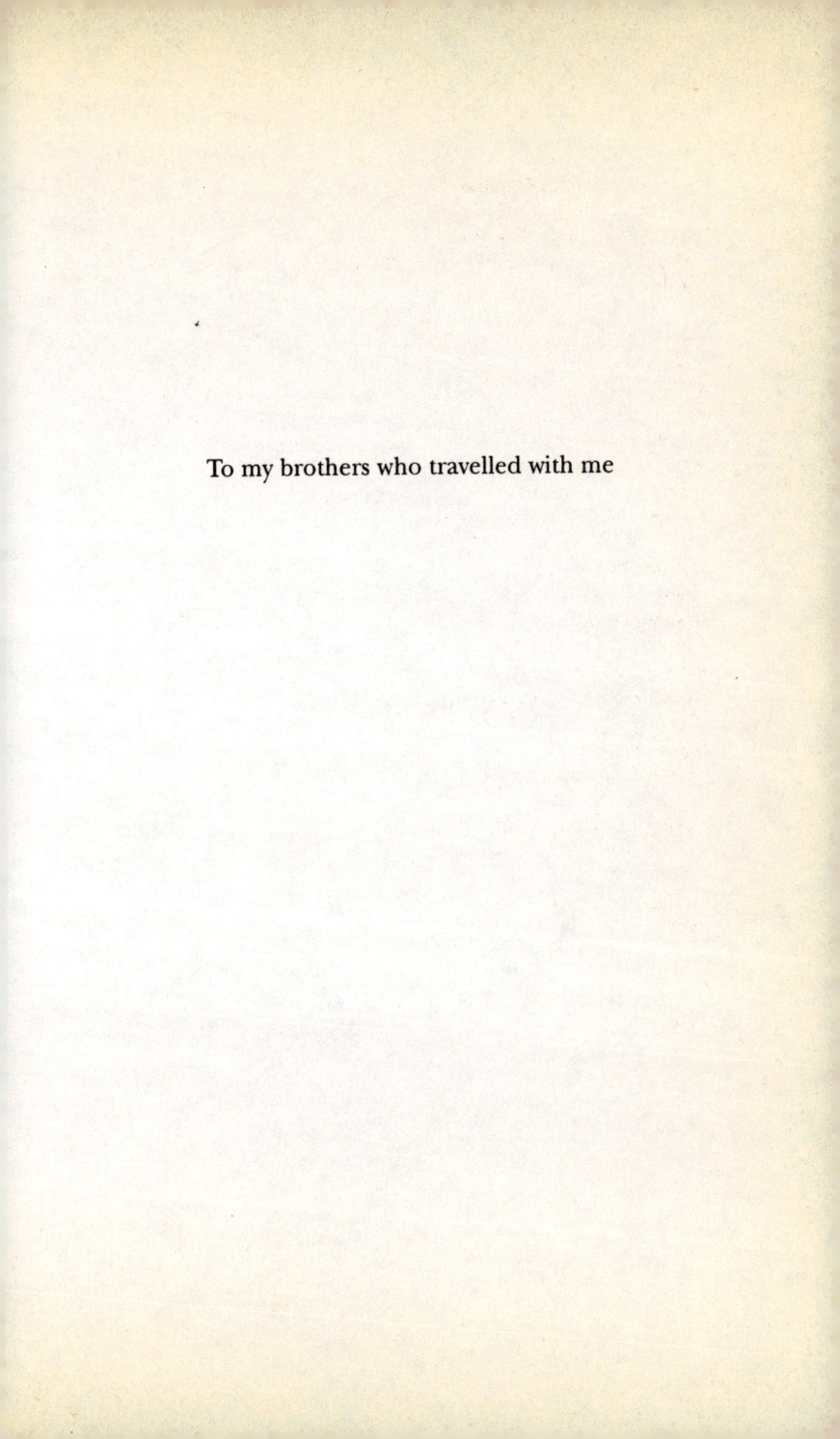

CONTENTS

Foreword ix

CHAPTER ONE
The Great Romance of Travel 1

CHAPTER TWO
From London to Tobruk 7

CHAPTER THREE
Hills or Flats 15

CHAPTER FOUR
A Sort of Home-coming 23

CHAPTER FIVE
Nightmare on Punt Street 35

CHAPTER SIX
The Ballad of Old Mick Dylan 43

CHAPTER SEVEN
The Day that God Slept In 51

CHAPTER EIGHT
Mountains to Hurdle, Horses to Toast 57

CHAPTER NINE
The Way Things Used to Be 67

CHAPTER TEN
Heroes 73

CHAPTER ELEVEN
Judgement Day 107

FOREWORD

If you had told me back in 1988 that eight years down the track I would be writing the foreword to Rupert's third book, I'd have thought you certifiable. 1988 was the year that Jason 'Rupert' McCall and I began our friendship as Colts at the Brothers Rugby Club. Since that time Rupert has managed to qualify in law, practise in law, and even break the law, on his way to being a full-time laureate.

Rupert's talents as a fledgling poet weren't always that obvious. In fact, to the 'boys down at Brothers' they were pretty much non-existent. We knew that he was an intelligent bloke because of the apparent ease with which he tackled his law studies, and we knew that he could run, pass and step with a rare passion. We were also acutely aware that he could sing along, albeit off key, to any number of Simon and Garfunkel or Bob Dylan melodies, but his real talent remained unearthed.

Years on, while his singing voice still searches for its ideal tone, Rupert has settled into the role of poet/writer quite naturally. Many of my team mates and I were initially surprised at his adeptness for poetry as he began churning out poem after poem for cause after cause. We were not surprised at the talent so much as by the fact that we had never witnessed it before.

It is with a great deal of pride that I now look back over the early stages of Rupert's journey. It is a pride shared by many of his friends in the man and manner in which he has played the hand he has been dealt. The way in which he has traded the high security of a budding legal career with the uncertain journey of a full-time poet. The fact that, essentially, he is the same self-effacing Rupert, with high ideals and family values, that we trained and played with in those early days.

Green & Gold Malaria is an extremely entertaining combination of poetry and literature. The book presents a young man during a phase of his journey through life. It highlights the humanity of his experience, the conflicts he faces, and the realisations he comes to. All of us, from the ninety-year-old grandmother to the six-year-old schoolboy, can relate to the images which he so clearly depicts.

FOREWORD

Even if read simply for the poetry, the book's offerings are both plentiful and varied. The journeys take you from the deserts of Tobruk to the cricket pitch in your own backyard, the racetracks of Ireland to the Margate TAB, and many places in between. Most moving of all, however, is Rupert's fierce pride in and loyalty towards everything that is Australian. This builds to an overwhelming crescendo with his last two poems, 'Green and Gold Malaria' and 'The Lucky Land'.

Now sit back and enjoy the read.

John Eales, Australian Wallaby Captain

Chapter One

The Great Romance of Travel

THE GREAT ROMANCE OF TRAVEL

The love that he had for his work was dying.

Although he didn't notice at first, he started to smile for the sake of it and conversation, despite being honest, became programmed enough to cause concern. He blamed the sun for waking him up in the morning and the moon for keeping him up at night. Then, when the words that guided him out of the woods began to suffocate his heart, he knew he had to leave.

The great romance of travel took a young bloke by the hand
To the dream of something better in an unknown foreign land.
The winds of autumn whispered for his spirit to belong
With an atmosphere he'd tasted in the lyrics of a song.
He packed his bag, he packed his flag, an old guitar as well.
The road would write the story that he knew he had to tell.
He counted down the days and still that song was on his brain,
Until the customs desk at Brisbane sent him out to meet his plane.
At last his soul was flying from a town of obligations.
At the point of no return . . . and he had no reservations.
The truth was out there somewhere, deep inside he knew it,
And if destiny was something real, then fate would bring him to it . . .

Whatever 'it' was, he was pretty sure that it couldn't be found in his current environment. His journey thus took on the nature of a modern-day hunting safari — an overseas adventure in search of the exotic truth — for that would certainly cure his weary mind.

Then it happened. As the jumbo skidded into Heathrow airport, London, his skin began to itch. It was only a minor irritation but annoying enough for him to consult a mirror within the terminal and notice a small rash forming on his neck. Nothing to worry about, he thought, remembering that the passenger beside him on the plane had been clumsy with his pepper sachet, ripping it open and spraying the stuff everywhere.

It certainly had been a long flight, but here he was in another country. What would it be like? Would Ash and Bear be waiting for him? What would they all do first?

A wild stampede of questions raced through his mind and, for now, the rash was forgotten.

THE GREAT ROMANCE OF TRAVEL

Chapter Two

From London to Tobruk

He knew the night was London when the stars above him snowed,
and he walked the famous crossing on the tar of Abbey Road.
He touched the block that chilled the flesh of many royal necks,
felt a dose of Ashes history that a tour of Lords injects.

London was everything it promised to be.

The great thing about this place was that every night tossed up a new adventure. He sipped a pint at The Rat and Parrot, whistled a tune at Waxy O'Connors, danced a jig at The Mean Fiddler, and still had a thousand pubs to choose from after that.

Every day was a history lesson in itself. A chilling wind accompanied tales told at The Tower of London, but as cold as it was, it had nothing on the icy stone block that saw many a queen's head roll.

He grew up believing that there were Eight Days a Week, so a brisk stroll over the crossing that made it onto The Beatles' last recorded album was considered very special. Not so special to the Abbey Road motorists held up to accommodate another tourist's photo.

Big Ben, Westminster Abbey, Piccadilly Circus, Oxford Circus, Leicester Square, Trafalgar Square, The Strand. In fact, he felt like a piece of plastic in a

Green & Gold Malaria

Monopoly set at one stage and he still hadn't passed 'Go'.

The ceilings of St Paul's Cathedral are awesome and the acoustics are such that on a quiet day, someone whispering at one end of the church can be heard at the other. A voice whispered that he should take the stairs down to the great hall of tombs. He wasn't sure why.

The answer came in the form of a plaque. It appeared similar to the countless other plaques on display, but this one meant something more to him and his brothers. It marked the resting place of Viscount Montgomery of Alamein KG, the World War II field commander under which his grandfather, Barney McCall, had fought.

He had always known that Barney was a Rat of Tobruk, a member of that legendary platoon of soldiers that sought shelter beneath the desert sand to escape the deadly bullet fire and hold off the advancing enemy. It had only been in recent years, however, that the shocking living conditions during those eight months were described to him, the special mateship of fellow diggers shared and the story of his grandfather's lucky escape told.

The bullet that struck Barney's helmet visor, peeling it apart like a sardine can before deflecting down into his left shoulder not far above his heart, was one that changed Barney's life. He lived to tell the tale, and his was one brave story of many that deserves our proud appreciation — an appreciation of the freedom that we live and breathe today.

THE HEROES OF TOBRUK

The soldier says a prayer as he breathes the desert air,
He shuts his eyes but knows he has to open them and look
At the war that he is in — it's a war he has to win,
It's a day that he'll remember — he has landed in Tobruk.

With survival on his mind and his loved ones left behind,
His enemy in front of him — his back against the seas.
The dust is up his nose — in his eyes and through his clothes,
The flies are never far and if they are, then it's the fleas.

There's nowhere he can go except the desert floor below,
So the digger earns his tag by doing just exactly that.
An inner strength is found as he burrows in the ground,
Then the sand becomes his shelter and the man becomes a rat.

From London To Tobruk

The only heat respite is in the chill that haunts the night.
He is hungry and the battle is forever in his ears.
But he doesn't know surrender — he's determined to defend 'er,
And his mates are there to laugh with him and take away his fears.

And the mateship lifts his hopes when they've got him on the ropes.
The boys are always there, although he knows he'll lose a few,
And the world seems rather grim, but he knows they died for him,
And it only makes him more the man to see the battle through.

The Rats refused to budge — it had been an eight-month trudge.
They defended what they had to with a spirit fierce and brave.
Then when news came through of peace and the bullet fire ceased,
The memories were something they would carry to their grave.

Now the soldier says a prayer for the ghosts he knows are there,
For the days that now are legend in the pages of a book,
And no matter where he's at, he is proud to be a Rat,
And we are just as proud of him — a hero of Tobruk.

Chapter Three

Hills or Flats

The past week had been one of the best in his life.

His younger brother, Boghead, fresh out of the Army Reserves, had saddled up beside him on the plane. Catching up with their other brother, Pooh Bear, in London ignited them all. Bear had been working there for twelve months and their reunion spelt danger in a land of pubs.

Clinking pint glasses with other Aussie friends, while toasting to anything from Lawson, Blaxland and Wentworth to John Dyson's catch back in 1981 put a constant smile on his face.

At the end of the week, he would be in Ireland and something told him that the fun wouldn't stop. Apparently they hated a drink and a good time over there. Before he donned the shamrock, however, he wanted to visit the home of cricket, the birthplace of the Ashes, the ground they all talked about — Lords.

Did you know that the only bloke to hit a straight six over the players' pavilion in the ground's history was an Aussie? Albert Trott did it back in 1899 and no tonk has been big enough since, although Lara came close once.

It was inspiration enough for him to purchase a cheap piece of willow on his way home and call his mates together the following day for a soul-stirring game of backyard cricket.

The boys obliged. In fact, they were loving it. A taped-up tennis ball, Bear keeping wicket, Tiger Sedgewick at first slip, big Ash in the gully, Lucas patrolling the covers, and an angry young Boghead steaming in off the long run-up, set the scene perfectly. Having won the toss, he elected to bat, of course, and noticing Mickster to be a bit shallow at mid-wicket, he was looking to go over the top.

Everything seemed fine on the surface, but something was seriously wrong. Don't worry — this team of young hopefuls was having an absolute ball, but there *was* something wrong. There was no backyard. They were playing on cold London concrete. There was no erratic cut or bounce off the pitch, no full-length dive to take a classic catch (unless you wanted to part with some skin), and no neighbour's dog to steal the ball after a misguided six and out.

It was definitely not as they remembered and reminisced.

Yesterday
(All My Troubles Seemed So Far Away)

When I sit and watch the cricket, there's a place I often go

Through a window where I stare upon a yard that needs a mow.

I am young again with brain cells that have not been faced with beer.

Although a few have left me now, the memories are clear.

Of a willow hurled in spirals to the call of hills or flats

By a kid who knows for certain — if he wins the toss, he bats.

On a track where something well pitched up

could whistle past your scone.

Where no man got out leg before, though nick behind was gone.

One hand off the house was fair, the road was six and out,

And the six was often worth it, if the fruit was there to clout.

'Hit the car — you're gone my friend! The shed is that way, son!'

In the name of backyard cricket, geez, we had some bloody fun!

And when you took the batting crease, you'd face like Brucey Laird,

Then you'd bowl and stare like Thommo, just to make the batsman scared.

You'd shout, 'Howzat!' like DK did and chew the gum like Viv.

There was nothing for the sake of dreams, a player wouldn't give.

To be bowled by one's own brother was the ultimate in shame,
And until you knocked his melon off, you hadn't cleared your name.
The skills involved in running called for commonsense and class.
As your partner crossed, you'd hit him with the perfect Gray Nic pass.

What a bat it was! The old quad scoop with cherries toe to handle,
And Kev, me neighbour, chucked, although it never caused a scandal.
The third ump wasn't heard of then, so close enough was in,
And to tamper with the tennis ball was not considered sin.

In fact, you'd always wrap the ball in tape to maximise the swing,
Then you'd let the perfect outy go and think that you were king.
The sun had gone down long ago, but still the blade would flash,
'One last ball, then up for tea' would herald one last bash.

Am I wrong or are we living in a 'caps on backwards' world?
Will our children soon be reading how the backyard bat was hurled?
Will blades of grass in future yards be strangers to our youth?
With every corner shop that dies, I'm closer to the truth.

But grief won't get me anywhere and nor will innuendo.
I know I must acknowledge that the game is on Nintendo.
Yesterday is written and will wipe away like chalk.
You can't ignore technology and who am I to talk?

For here I am on Sunday with my hand on a remote.
The grass outside will stay that long, unless I buy a goat,
So I think I'll tape the old ball up and mow meself a wicket,
Then I'll ring the boys . . .
The square's prepared, let's play ourselves some cricket!

The boys knew it too.

Tiger looked at Bear. Bear looked at Ash who, in turn, looked at Lucas. Lucas looked at Mickster. Mickster looked at Boghead. As Boghead's eyes met his, he felt a bit of a tingle in his neck and started scratching at it. That bloody itch was back! But now it seemed to have spread to his left shoulder. He'd have to do something about it before it got worse.

Then he witnessed something that could only be described as bizarre. As he stood at the batting crease, planning where to dispatch his next boundary, he noticed something strange about the fieldsmen. Every one of them.

They were all scratching.

Chapter Four

A Sort of Homecoming

A Sort of Home-coming

In Dublin's fair city, where the girls are so pretty,
I first set my eyes on sweet Molly Malone.
She wheeled her wheelbarrow through streets broad and narrow,
Selling cockles and mussels, alive alive oh!

(Traditional)

Like so many Australians before him, a home-coming sort of feeling swept through his heart as he stood on Irish soil in front of Molly Malone's statue. A little way down the road, he met another statue, the qualifications of which read 'novelist, poet and patriot'.

He had come, not only to drink Guinness with the local leprechauns, but to trace the history of his great uncle, Richard Roche of Cork. Richard was of the Irish rebel breed branded moonlighters and when he got sick and tired of pouring boiling water on peasant-bashing landlords, he came to Queensland and set up a farm in Warwick. He then paid for his brothers and sisters to follow and it was his little brother, Cornelius, who would father Ellen Roche (who married grandfather Barney McCall of Chapter Two fame).

Now he stood where his great uncle once rebelled. That part of his blood which was Irish pumped proudly and furiously as he eyed the statue in front of him like an old friend. He would meet plenty of old friends in the next few weeks.

Lost Souls

Everywhere I travel in this pub-infested place,
From Waterford to Galway Bay and back,
I see a lot of statues and they stare me in the face,
Another lost soul coming down the track.

A novelist, a patriot, a poet in my sight,
It's hard to think they once were mortal men.
For the stone entrenches mystery that idle print can't write,
And wisdom chipped by chisel, not by pen.

Does he doubt my own intelligence or laugh at what I write?
Is he quick to list the qualities I lack?
Will his shadow come to haunt me in the middle of the night?
Another lost soul coming down the track.

A SORT OF HOME-COMING

And what a mighty track it is that stretches to the past,
To men that bled the blood that I bleed now,
On a strange familiar land that I've discovered now at last,
I am home, aye — I am home, I am . . . somehow.

Dicky Roche where are ya mate? I know you'd be with us.
A rebel proud, you didn't cop their flak,
But injustice broke your spirit, so you caught the Warwick bus.
Another lost soul coming down the track.

The pride that never left you has been handed down to me,
And verses I have written in my heart,
A heart that longs for nourishment from sunburnt land and sea,
For that is where my journeys always start.

And I stare back at the statue and the stone within his eyes,
A mortal man who rose above the pack.
And I think I would have known him, for a statue never lies,
Another lost soul coming down the track.

Lost souls is an understatement.

There they were — driving down the road, knowing full well that the last exit taken was the wrong exit. On the wrong end of another big

GREEN & GOLD MALARIA

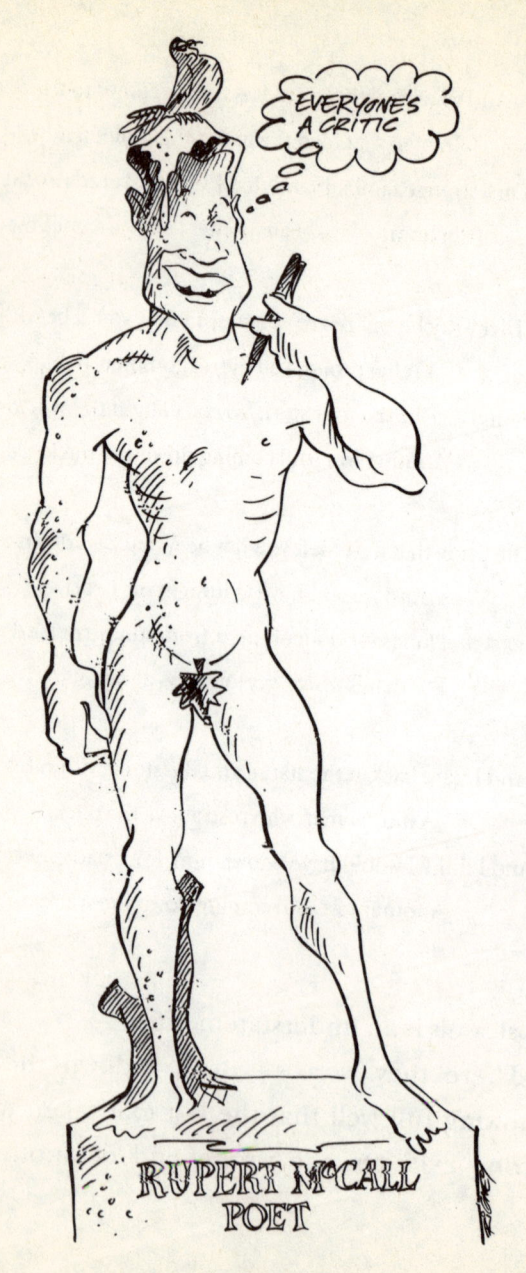

night in Dublin and heading to Cork with a hangover. The three brothers who had been living in each other's pockets for the last three weeks were lost, with headaches, and maps were flying everywhere. That's a bad combination in any brother's language.

Finally the navigator got his act together and the boys were back on the N7 with a full head of steam. The brotherly sledge-fest ceased, although the car remained silently snaky.

It was Bear who snapped the John Williamson tape out of his collection and slipped it into the car stereo. From then on, they might as well have been heading across the Nullarbor. Willo's voice was the best headache tablet he had ever taken. And the brothers? Well, they were one again.

THE BALLAD OF GOOD AUSSIE WILLO

The tape was in and play was pressed,

You took us out of Dublin.

You gave us half a chance to break away.

For every blade of farmyard grass,

And every tree we saw to pass,

Was just a bit Australian for that second of the day.

The Kildare people dipped their lids,

And wished us well in wave,

I wish they could have been inside the car.

I wish they could have heard you sing

That Cootamundra Wattle thing,

I wish they could have climbed aboard and heard your sweet guitar.

Willo — you're a legend, mate,

I don't know how you do it.

Every time you give me old Bob's tale,

I think about his sorrow,

And I look towards tomorrow,

A knowing tear will find my face and in my heart, they wail.

A Sort Of Home-Coming

John Williamson

Then we hit a place called Portaloise,

Sounded French to me.

But bombs were out of mind at this fine hour,

'Cos my soul was back on Uluru,

Sailing down the Kakadu,

I do believe the rock has given you its special power.

And me and Bear and Boghead,

Brothers more alike than most,

We were howling down the highway with the dingo.

We shaved our heads to travel,

Down the winding Irish gravel,

I s'pose we're wild colonials and all because of Ringo.

You took us through to Fethard,

And a feed of pumpkin soup,

In a pub that served its schooners black and wet.

And of freckles, we had fewest,

But we were truest, we were bluest.

We were hummin' — you were strummin' — it's a day I won't forget.

As they bid farewell to Fethard, young Boghead was heard from the back to say, 'Hey, Bear. Pull over at the next chemist you see, mate. I've gotta' get something for this damned rash.'

He just nodded and sang an extra verse of 'True Blue' to himself.

Chapter Five

Nightmare on Punt Street

He remembered the day Bear guaranteed him he could double his money by backing the first favourite at Wangaratta — an attractive proposition for a bored law student doing it tough on Austudy.

Since that first trip to the Margate TAB, his love affair with racing had blossomed and inspired him to write lines like:

> *There's something great that separates this grand old sport of kings,*
> *Of queens as well, as Gai would tell, and many other things.*
> *This world of ours is changing, there is no denying that.*
> *You sometimes have to ask yourself exactly where it's at,*
> *But when the photo's been developed and correct weight's*
> *been declared,*
> *When we reminisce the memories and the magic that we've shared,*
> *When, once again, those brilliant creatures pass us in their game,*
> *The tears we cry in pain or glory all come out the same.*
> *And when the book of turf is written and those tears fall on its pages,*
> *The story told may well grow old, but the legend never ages.*
>
> (Extract from 'The Legend Lives On', 1996)

You see, it had gone beyond a money thing for him. Sure, he still enjoyed picking the odd box trifecta and kicking home the odd favourite, but the shiver up his spine when 'like scissors through paper' Super Impose 'cut through the pack' to win the 1991 Epsom Handicap, meant he had fallen for the sport.

Why then was he sitting in a smoky Ladbroke's betting shop in Limerick investing his precious Irish pounds on steeplechasing nags he didn't know anything about? That was the punt side of it. That was the vision of doubling his Guinness money for the night. That was the greatest tragedy of all when every one-paced flea he backed that day seemed to have only one gear in the straight, i.e. reverse (that was, if they hadn't fallen already).

He slumped back in his chair. As the drone of the caller's voice lulled his tired mind into a semi-coma, he closed his eyes and wished he was that student back in the Margate TAB again. Yep, it was definitely much easier to pick a winner there.

Nightmare on Punt Street

The Margate TAB and Me

A lovely sunny Monday morn it was down Margate way —
So beautiful, so bliss, it was a public holiday.
The butcher birds were singing as the sunlight filtered through
To a place where I was smiling and the sky above was blue.
There was something in the air that made it great to be alive.
Was there something in the hurdle at 11:55?
That question would be answered with a morning paper flip,
A three-page turn with speed to burn and then the sacred rip.
My mother lodged a protest as I galloped out the door.
She asked where I was heading, though I think she knew the score.
'The beach would be ideal,' she said. 'The Scarborough surf is pumping,
And they tell me down at Woody Point the yellow tail are jumping,
Or how about a picnic? You could take the dog and me.'
But she knew the day was perfect for the Margate TAB.

Would the boys be there professing that today they had the goods?
Is the Pope a Roman Catholic? Does a bear shit in the woods?
For if Sunday was a day of rest to pray the holy Sabbath,
Today would be a day of punt to play the holy Tabbath.
There was Windross with his laffer curve — a punter from the south,
The Wilson boy from Clontarf — he could read the horse's mouth.
Douglas loved the punt as much as life and lunch itself.
His knack of backing winning nags was something off the shelf.

Springbok Barker's tips were like a sip of fine red wine.

Hickton was on welfare till he joined this other line.

Tricky Dicky McIlwain would always come along,

With a certain late-mail special — he was very rarely wrong,

And I, of course, could smell a horse, I never backed a flea.

We were pretty well the legends of the Margate TAB.

From Muswellbrook to Eagle Farm, from Murray Bridge to Sale,

Every horse was analysed from lugging bit to tail.

Our expertise was blended and it ended with a system

That was sure to find the winners, no, we never, ever missed 'em!

So I emptied out my wallet — every dollar, every cent,

And in temporary fashion, said goodbye to all my rent.

The ink, it smelt of money as it filled the sacred squares.

The patrons were in awe of us, it echoed in their stares.

Barker made the run because at nights he worked security,

And there were many who would die to see the secret of our surety.

Tickets through the terminal, now everything was sweet.

Barring something drastic, soon the job would be complete.

I couldn't think of anywhere my arse would rather be

Than the chair where I was sitting in the Margate TAB.

If he had of got out earlier, he would have won for sure.

If the silly, bloody jockey knew what flamin' whips were for.

If the trainer had him fitter, then he would have made the trip.
If we'd just ignored the bloke next door, who mouthed that bloody tip.
If he had a better barrier, the mongrel would have won.
If I'se on board the bastard, then I know what I'd have done.
If a lot of things were different, then it wasn't hard to see,
We would have taken millions from the Margate TAB.

I left, not with my rent, but with a sense of déjà vu.
The week before, I'd left this place and felt this sickness too.
As I checked the ground for fallen coins and made my sorry way,
I thought of all the places where I should have gone that day.
My mother she'd be waiting and I knew she'd pull the whip,
When I asked her for a loan, I thought of pieces she would strip,
So when she gave me fifty bucks, I thought she must be on the nectar!
But apparently at Eagle Farm she'd scooped a big trifecta.
'How'd ya manage that?' I said, my pride shot down in flames.
She said, 'I've got this real good system, son — I pick them on their names.'
'Twas then I made the promise that I'd never punt again,
I'd never waste my time and cash with all those desperate men.
But don't be fooled — come Saturday you know where I will be —
I'll be back to get that million from the Margate TAB.

Snapping out of his coma, he cursed that first favourite at Wangaratta. If only it had come second.

Chapter Six

The Ballad of Old Mick Dylan

The Ballad of Old Mick Dylan

Kilkenny was a great little town.

The accommodation they managed to snavel was a bedroom on top of a corner shop. It reminded him of Arthur Fonzarelli's apartment in 'Happy Days' — and happy days they were!

When the closing bell rang at the pub next door to the Pumphouse, the locals called for Mick. Well, old Mick put paid to his pint in just one stride, then stood up to sing the song he had been singing at about 11.30 p.m. ever since they could remember.

He expected 'Danny Boy', but instead was mesmerised by a beautiful rendition of 'Blowin' in the Wind' sung in eerie silence on a cold Irish night. Not one glass clinked as the locals joined Mick in the chorus.

How many times must a man look up before he sees the sky?
How many ears must one man have before he can hear people cry?
How many deaths will it take till he knows that too many people have died?

A twenty-one-year-old Bob Dylan had written the song that had brought the night to a standstill. What a freak, he thought.

Culture of that kind was mixed with culture of another — a tour of Kilkenny Castle the next morning. Ireland is a land of castles. Many of them lie in ruins, but this one had been restored almost to perfection (except for the smoke alarms and surveillance cameras, which he didn't imagine were around during early century battles). There was even a ghost or two still hanging around.

One single room in the castle resembled an entire art gallery. He could only stand there and look up in awe at the size of the portraits. The bloke who painted some of these must have dead-set used a ladder! The age of them made him realise how young his home country was, and the quality was magnificently inspiring, even in the artless eyes of a rookie.

Wait a minute! Did someone say rookie? Didn't they know of his experience when it came to splashing the old paintbrush? Didn't they know of his brilliant expertise when it came to some of the great artists in history? Didn't they know he had opened the Caboolture Arts and Crafts Show in 1995?

The Ballad of Old Mick Dylan

AN ODE TO ART

You know, I've always been an art buff —

An art buff from the start,

So when they kindly asked me

if I'd write an ode to art,

Green & Gold Malaria

I said, 'That will not be a problem',
And to paint the picture clearer,
My old mates back in art school
called me Rupert Namatjira,
And I love that bloke — Picasso,
And I'm up with Rembrant too.
His reds were always bettered
by his lighter shades of blue.

And then there's Michelangelo,
that Sistine Chapel freak.
When you wind up painting ceilings,
things are looking pretty bleak.
But I've gotta give Mike credit, folks,
The job he did was swell,
with a lot of bloody Taubmans,
and a neck complaint as well.

And that other bloke Van Morrison —
No what's-his-name? Van Gogh!
He sharpened up the pocket knife
And took the ear right off.
And what about the pastel prince,
That moustached mogul — Done.
In the finger-painting hall of fame,
He's standing on his own.

THE BALLAD OF OLD MICK DYLAN

Now I ask, does tinned spaghetti

have a place in modern art?

Well, it does if you're familiar

with that maniac Pro Hart.

I was eating dinner with my girlfriend

when I saw him on the telly,

Sliding through a painting

on his big, fat, hairy belly.

Jelly, spag, tomato sauce,

he squished it semi-nude.

The end result was brilliant,

though it put us off our food.

But that abstract stuff amazes me,

I just can't work it out.

Just before I studied one,

and then without a doubt,

I said 'I reckon this one's easy,

It's a tablecloth with checks'

Then the artist comes along

and says, 'They're dolphins having sex!'

'Fair enough' I thought,

I mean I've never seen them do it,

So good luck to the dolphin pervert

lunatic who drew it!

Green & Gold Malaria

From this ode I think it's obvious,
It must be clear to you,
That when it comes to art analysis,
I haven't got a clue.
'Yes, he'd better stick to poetry'
is what you'd all be hopin',
So, in rhyming verse, I now declare
This arts and crafts show open!

Chapter Seven

The Day that God Slept In

He sang the song of Cardiff, 'Bread of Heaven, Wales Forever',
At Lansdowne Road he belted out a verse of 'Nae, No, Never'.
Dublin turned to publin in the days that followed that,
On bar room stools from Tommy Wrights to Scruffy Murphs, he sat.
He sailed the ring of Kerry and he scaled the Cliffs of Moher,
He drank the brown in Galway town and toasted to the pour.
He kissed the stone at Blarney and he saw Killarney's splendour,
Then he marched the streets of Belfast, reading signs of 'no surrender'.

You can spend a long time visiting, admiring and enjoying some of the most magnificent visions of natural beauty that this world has to offer and then wake up one morning not understanding any of it.

That day would dawn on him in a little Irish town called Athlone. An unexplainable craziness that ended in the loss of sixteen young innocent lives and their teacher. There was nothing they could do.

Standing at the bar on that cold afternoon, they stared at another television newsflash as if caught in some sort of trance. There was nothing they could say.

As a tear rolled down the old publican's face, a sudden feeling of homesickness came over him. That's where he wanted to be at that moment — safe in his room and away from all of this. He knew, however, that sooner or later he would have to walk outside and face the sheer confusion of a world that sometimes spins just a little bit too fast — a world where too many answers were blowin' in a cold Kilkenny wind at about 11.30 p.m. every night.

THE DAY THAT GOD SLEPT IN

The IRA was asked today to please restore the peace,
But they want theirs as well and so I doubt the bombs will cease.
Snipers ride to suicide in long, uncivil wars,
Holy city murder for a not so holy cause.
But today I read the paper and the chill became intense,
The sun shines on our doorstep but today it makes no sense.
I am many miles away but still I can't conceal my pain,
And the world is crying with me now for Dunblane.

A man shot down in Dublin town — the crime rate's getting bad,
And roast beef's off the menu since the British cows went mad.
Di's been forced to get divorced, the Queen's been stalked again,
An AIDS-infected angel takes out twenty-seven men.
But today I read the story of a world in disarray,
The words were there in black and white, but everything was grey.
An evil waste of innocence and how do you explain
The day that God slept in up there in Dunblane.

'Screams of terror', said the Mirror, 'tore the day in half',
The old man's eyes are tired, they've forgotten how to laugh.
The young man frowns, his music drowns, the woman's face is snow,
But the child she holds is smiling . . . well, I guess he doesn't know.
He cannot read the headlines — how his fellow comrades fell,
For once in all my tears and years, I hope that there's a hell.
And I read it, and I read it, but I'm reading it in vain,
For I'll never understand that day in Dunblane.

Chapter Eight

Mountains to Hurdle, Horses to Toast

Mountains to Hurdle, Horses to Toast

On a cold Croaghpatrick Mountain peak, he stood in awesome solace,
He smiled at Stirling Castle in the name of William Wallace.
He danced upon the woodwork where The Beatles once rehearsed,
Then he heard the roar at Aintree as the horses jumped the first.

Irish pilgrims put on their climbing boots and arm themselves with rosary beads one Sunday every year to scale Croaghpatrick Mountain, in honour of St Patrick's snake-chasing feat many centuries ago.

English punters put on their pin-striped suits and arm themselves with form guides one Saturday every year to attend Aintree, Liverpool, in honour of thirty-odd hurdle-happy horses in an event known as the Grand National.

From one track to the other, and Scotland in between, he travelled, his soul soaking up the sights with the hope of keeping them there forever, should he not return. His skin irritation had worsened, despite the ointment prescribed by a chemist in Limerick and, although he didn't let it affect his adventures, it started to worry him. Fortunately there were no signs of the rash as he stood among Aussie friends in a beer tent on Grand National day.

Atmosphere was oozing from every fancy hat and pumping from every punter's smile for a race that should be titled Survival of the Fittest. For the horses that are left standing when they hit the home straight, it will have taken approximately nine minutes to fly over thirty fences, which stand as big as the horses themselves. If your horse is

Mountains to Hurdle, Horses to Toast

unlucky enough to fall at the first, then it's a longer race still, and even if he's cleared the last, there's an invisible brick wall waiting somewhere for him in the straight, which he may hit through sheer exhaustion. Many a story is told of the poor nag that was twenty lengths clear with only thirty metres to go, but who refused to taste the glory of Grand National victory by applying the brakes and calling it a day — much to the dismay of those punters who carried his name on their ticket.

'It's harder to pick than the Melbourne Cup!' cried Hairy Dog McKenzie, his face buried in the form guide. Down a few pounds already, Big Chundy couldn't have agreed more.

'Melbourne Cup' was all Tiger Sedgewick needed to hear. He was a racing enthusiast from way back and, getting sentimental, proposed a toast to that first Tuesday in November, before reminiscing some of its great victors.

Names were flying thick and fast, from the very first to the very last . . .

THE DREAM

A horse, a dream, nothing more, and nothing less is needed,
But somewhere down that endless straight, the weaker beasts are weeded.
The old man watched the young man pass, admiring his horse,
He couldn't help but ask as to the boy's intended course,
For stranger sights he'd witnessed in the years before this hour,
But something made him want to know the fate of David Power.
A boy who, if he held a fear, he didn't let it show,
'Three hundred miles I've come,' he said. 'Three hundred miles to go.
And, Mister, let me tell you why I saddled this bloke up —
I'm on me way to Flemington to win meself a cup.

Mountains to Hurdle, Horses to Toast

The Melbourne Cup!' he added, with a fire in his eyes.
'I reckon this bloke's good enough to take away the prize,
And when I steer him past the post, these dusty thirsty miles
Will then become a river filled with glory, gold and smiles,
And, in my ears, the doubts and jeers that echoed our departure
Will then become a sea of cheers, a sea of cheers for Archer.'
The old man winked as if to say, 'I hope ya get there, son'
But what he didn't know was that the dream had just begun . . .

As they reach the line, the big blokes home, it's Archer for the first!
And here's the mighty Phar Lap with his red cyclonic burst!
Now Peter Pan was twice the man, he must have been a goer,
And didn't TJ love the call of 'Here comes Toparoa!'
Galilee was brilliant as the bookies ducked for cover.
'Show me the Cup, then double me up!' said Johnson on Rain Lover.
Harry White was Thinking Big, and so was Mr Cummings,
And when the heavens opened up, the Cup was Van Der Humming.
I can hear the punters cheering for the charge of Gold And Black,
And step aside 'cos here comes Arwon streaking through the pack.
Hyperno heard them roaring and he answered every call,
A hundred out, it's Hayesy's shout, they won't catch Beldale Ball!
Just A Dash explodes away! He's just a shade too good,
Gurner's Lane in '82 with Dittman scraping wood.
The race has proven nature wrong 'cos Kiwi sure did fly!
The bold Black Knight was in full flight with victory in his eye.

What a finish, neck and neck, but What A Nuisance kicks!
At Talaq would streak the pack in 1986.
Now look at Kensei on the rails with Olsen sitting cosy,
And nothing in the racing world was gonna stop big Rosy!
Freedman's time in '89 was nothing but Tawrrific,
Kingston Rule was sitting cool with Beadman's smile prolific.
Let's Elope has kicked away and Bart's a nine Cup hero,
Then in the rain, the old grey train, you little beaut, Subzero!
They'll fill the Cup with Guinness for the awesome Vintage Crop,
And Jeune would score in '94 with Harris proud on top.
Oliver was steering home a detonated scud,
When Doriemus screamed to victory by blasting through the mud…

Every jockey, every trainer, every owner's dream
Is to have their horse inducted in the caller's winning scream,
And nothing will be different when they take the yard this year —
The ladies in their fancy hats, the punters in their cheer,
The course in all its colour and the butterflies knee deep,
The buck each way you hope will pay, the good old classroom sweep.
Counting down the seconds for the Melbourne Cup to start,
With a ticket in your pocket and a time bomb in your heart.
The runners quickly loaded in a quest for life or death,
The starter holds the button and the country holds its breath…

Then somewhere down that endless straight, a horse will see the line,
His ears will pin and deep within, she'll whisper, 'This one's mine!'
The rest they say is history, another horse is through
On that Tuesday in November, in the race where dreams come true.

Was that a tear in Tiger Sedgewick's eye? It appeared to him that old Sedge was shedding a tear and he hadn't even blown his money on the big one yet. He would have lent some comfort to his fellow punter if he hadn't broken out in an attack of the shivers himself. That bloody rash was back!

Strange days indeed.

BART AND T.J.

Chapter Nine

The Way Things Used to Be

The Way Things Used To Be

There hadn't been too many days when he'd missed the law. In fact, sitting on a Sunday afternoon train back to London after a big weekend in Liverpool, he couldn't recall any.

Twenty months earlier, he left the family law files piled high on his desk, never to return. The next morning he brushed his teeth for the first time in his life as a full-time poet. The toothpaste tasted so much different as it polished the shine on a huge smile.

The decision to make this transition had provided him with countless opportunities, including the one that had now taken him to the other side of the globe. It had also dealt its fair share of days when he wondered whether it was all worth it. At the end of these days, he would go to sleep telling himself over and over that it *was* worth it, and wake up with no regrets at all.

That feeling remained with him the next day when, on the promise of lunch, he walked into his brother's London office sensing a nine-to-five atmosphere almost immediately. Not that that was an inherently bad concept; it just reminded him of the way things used to be.

There was something familiar in the coffee that

the receptionist made him. Something reminiscent in the way his brother's secretary reeled off a quick succession of photocopies. Something beautiful in the reassurance given to his brother that she would cover for him if he was late back to the office and a tad under the weather. Some things he did miss after all.

THE SECRETARYLESS BLUES

There's a rumour going 'round the place — I'm not sure if you know it,
But I gave away my law career to be a full-time poet.
You see, I couldn't cop the nine-to-five, my life was such a bore,
My nights were often sleepless and I hated family law.
The phone became my enemy, for many was the wife
Or the husband who would grace me with the story of their life.

Now I live without that horror — I've escaped the office cell,
And I won't be going back, but there is something I must tell.
There is something that I long for — it's the one thing that I miss,
Like the sleep-inducing softness of a mother's goodnight kiss.
'Twas the shining light that stood behind my each and every file.
'Twas the unashamed beauty of my secretary's smile.

How I wish that it was here again to never, ever fade.
How I wish that I could sip again, the coffee that she made.
For when darkness falls upon me and my writing hand grows weary,
I think of how she typed for me and get a little teary.
Her fingers used to sparkle as they danced across the keys.
They were faster than a hungry mouse in search of fallen cheese.

And when my foolish ways with alcohol resulted in a morning
When my head was like a speedway with a mouth forever yawning.
When a dose of pre-lunch silence seemed a more attractive choice
Than the monotonal onslaught of a client's whingeing voice,
She would pounce upon that telephone and follow up her greeting
With a 'Sorry, Mr So and So. Right now he's in a meeting.'

As a fax machine exponent, she is standing on her own.
A better photocopier, I've never, ever known.
She could open up a letter with a flicker of the wrist,
And her word-processing magic will be very sorely missed.
Now like a lightning-struck antenna, like a car without an aerial,
My life has no reception of the kind that's secretarial.

Sometimes you don't appreciate the wicket that you're on
Until the players that are helping you have packed their bags and gone.
So I send this little message to the bosses of the world:
Before you choose to criticise, before abuse is hurled,
Before you spit the dummy and before you do ya cherry,
Just think of how your life would be without a secretary.

Chapter Ten

Heroes

Soccer was one game that he had never got excited about.

Why then was he standing at the Royal Oak, knee deep in beer, with adrenalin pumping through his veins? The game that had captivated him was one played between Newcastle United and Liverpool and in his own terms, this had been an absolute cracker. From one–nil to one all, two–one, two all, three–two to three all, the evenly divided pommy-packed pub was ready to explode going into extra time.

Stan Collymore's miracle left-foot screamer left Newcastle fans mortified beyond belief. Personally, he had become a Liverpool fan in recent weeks and was glad in a way that his old soccer-playing mates, whom he had bagged on many occasions, weren't there to see him jumping around like a lunatic with a classic double air punch.

In the celebrations that followed, he realised something that he should have realised months before, sitting at the Nelson Mandella-inspired opening ceremony of the All Blacks *v.* Springboks World Cup rugby final with tears streaming down his face. The more he travelled, the more he was convinced that sport was sport and whatever sport you watched with whatever players at whatever level, the factors contributing to a great sporting spectacle, i.e. the confrontation, the skill, the courage, the pain and the glory, were the same in any sport lover's language.

The excitement must have stirred him up because later that night he had the strangest dream. It was a tangled web of those who belonged in the club to which Stan Collymore had just been inducted — The Heroes.

BALLAD OF A FREAK

I absolutely love it when the circus comes to town —
The animals and acrobats, the antics of a clown.
There's fire-breathing jugglers and lion-taming feats,
And generally the kind of acts that put the bums on seats.
But forget the bearded lady and the human cannon-ball,
I do believe my eyes have seen the greatest freak of all,
And folk will come from every corner just to have a squiz,
To cheer him when he takes the ball, to hear his knuckles fizz.
The batsman taking strike can sense that death is very near,
As his mates prepare his coffin in a dressing-room of fear,
For their fate is in his fingers, each a weapon in itself.
One slip and you'll be read as a statistic on the shelf.
Like a cobra poised to kill his prey with any grip he likes,
Let us analyse his venom and observe the way he strikes:
The leggy is a vicious tool, which devastates the batting,
And it stuns its helpless victims, as we saw with Mr Gatting.

And beware the dreaded toppy as it bites the pitch and jumps —
    It will paralyse its victim, then demoralise his stumps.
    But the king of all deliveries — the 'little bloody ripper'
Is the leather-clad phenomenon that cricket calls The Flipper.

Just look into the victim's eyes and note his gaze of terror,
    As it skids beneath a bat too late to resurrect its error.
    The Sheik of Tweak has struck again! A hero has been born,
And the pages of the record books will feel the ink of Warne.

    I'm older now but still I'm like a kid again this week,
'Cos the big top comes to Brisbane and it brings this spinning freak,
    And so I bid you don the zinc and make your journey down,
    Roll up! Roll up! Ye cricket fans — the circus is in town.

(Written after Shane Warne's amazing Test hat trick against England in Melbourne, January 1995.)

THE LIFE OF RILEY

I remember what she said, there was something in her head,
In her legs and in her arms and in her heart.
It was something made of fire, with ambition and desire —
She was ready now to take the world apart.

The training was behind her, still the critics would remind her
Of the soul-destroying consequence of failure,
But standing on the blocks, well, forget the voice that knocks —
She was swimming for herself and for Australia.

And the Games now hold the story of Samantha's triple glory,
The flash of gold reflected in her smile.
Then her Aussie heart was hurled at the countries of the world
For a victory in record-breaking style,

And that something in her head, in the sweat and tears she shed,
That something that would see her make the team,
Was alive in every stroke, in every record that she broke —
That something was Samantha Riley's dream.

(Written after the World Championships of swimming in 1995.)

Green & Gold Malaria

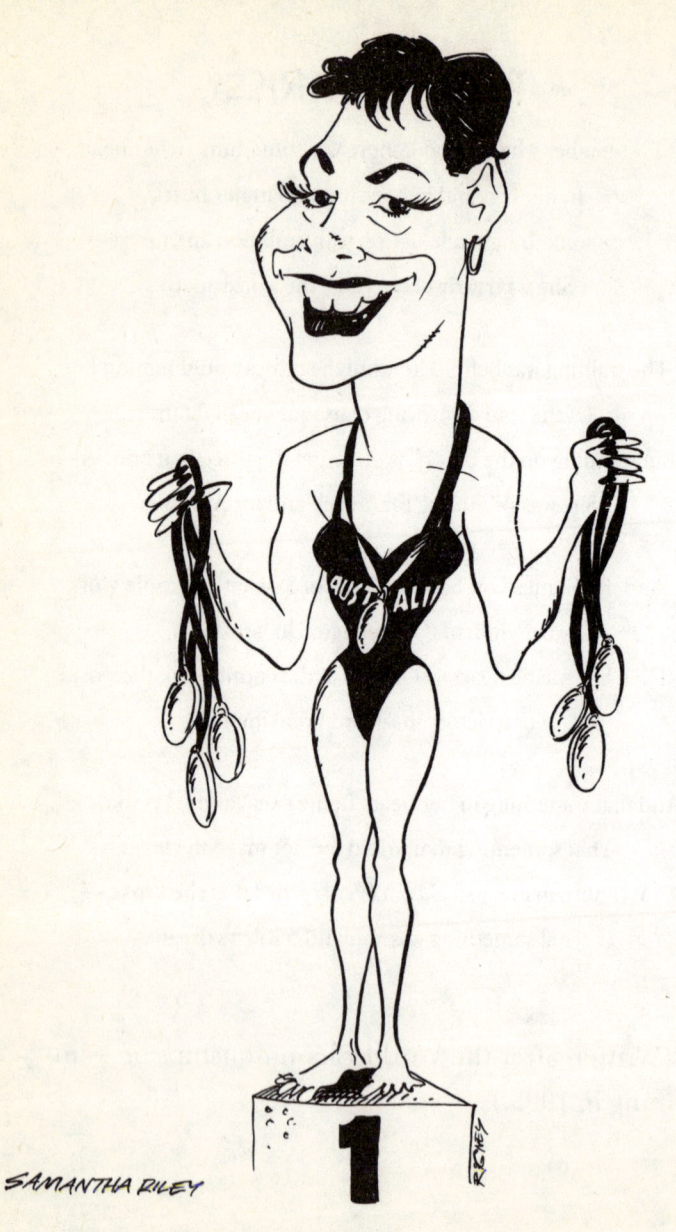

SAMANTHA RILEY

HEROES

ODE TO A RED DOG

Now he doesn't go for knee-length strides, he doesn't shave his melon.

He doesn't throw his racquet or resort to courtside yellin'.

He hasn't got the biggest serve, he isn't six foot four.

He's not a baseline basher 'cos he reckons that's a bore.

I doubt you'll ever seem him in a million-dollar ad,

But he's the greatest ad for sportsmanship the game has ever had.

And he might not win the final, but he shouldn't have to, should he?

'Cos he's a proud and brave Australian, and that'll do me, Woody.

(Written after Mark Woodforde defeated Thomas Enqvist to make it through to the semi-final of the 1996 Australian Open.)

Green & Gold Malaria

MARK WOODFORDE

The Whale-regurgitated Kiwi versus the Great Spring-heeled Eel

The face of little Rosco told the whole depressing tale,

As tragic as a postie with an empty sack of mail.

His old man called him over. 'Rosco, grab yaself a knee,

And tell ya Dad exactly what the problem seems to be.'

Well, the little bloke inhaled as if the news was catastrophic,

Then he told of how at school they had a new assignment topic.

'Now, come on, son,' the old man said, 'assignments aren't so bad!'

Rosco snapped, 'Well, this one is — it's gonna drive me mad!

"Here's one for the sports fans," said our teacher Mr Bugby,

"A seven-minute oral on the greatest man in rugby."'

His dad let loose, 'Ya silly goose! There's nothing wrong with that!

I sometimes flamin' wonder if I'm bringing up a cat!'

'Ah, pull ya head in, Poppy — let me give the wider view.

There's this Kiwi in our class and he's a bloody big one too.

I've never really liked him 'cos he thinks he's pretty tough,

He bashes kids at recess time and all that kinda stuff.

And I know he'll speak on Jonah 'cos he's got the same cold stare,

He palms off grade one students and he's dreadlocked half his hair,

And this was one assignment where I aimed to top the class.

Instead, that giant Kiwi's gonna put me on me arse!'

Green & Gold Malaria

Jonah Lomu

HEROES

Inspired by his rugby days, the old man went himself,
'See that Oxford Dictionary sitting on the shelf?'
The youngster winced as if to cop the standard 'work hard' spiel,
But to his surprise, the old man whispered, 'Go and look up "eel".'
Well, assignment day arrived and yes, they came in droves for Jonah.
The Kiwi was his biggest fan but certainly no loner.
They raved about his size and strength and some gave demonstrations,
And then it came to Rosco for the final presentation.
He opened up a Bible and he read to them this tale:
'Now Jonah was disgorged from the stomach of a whale,
Yeah, spewed up by a fish! And while the truth's a little shoddy,
An eel's a slippery species, with an elongated body.
That, my friends, is quoted from a dictionary source,
But there's more to eels that make it onto rugby fields, of course.
For in order to survive, he has developed other features,
In the lineout he gets higher up than any other creature.
Then with massive hands and fingers, he engulfs the flying ball,
To present it to his forwards for the perfect rolling maul.
With a hint of Michael Jordan in his fingertip control,
And a touch of Michael Lynagh in the boot that kicks his goals,
He can run and he can pass, and he can tackle like a demon.'
By now the class was on its feet and everyone was screamin'!
'Cos with footage from the Super 12 which featured all his latest,
The cry went up for 'Ealesy!' Yes — they thought he was the greatest.

So Rosco topped the class and, well, the Kiwi, he was cactus.
Then at lunch-time all the kids went out and did some lineout practice,
Which only goes to demonstrate, no matter how one feels,
You can put high heels on Jonah, but still he's not as tall as Eales.

(Written during John Eales' remarkable Super 12 Series in 1996, an effort that was rewarded with the captaincy of his country.)

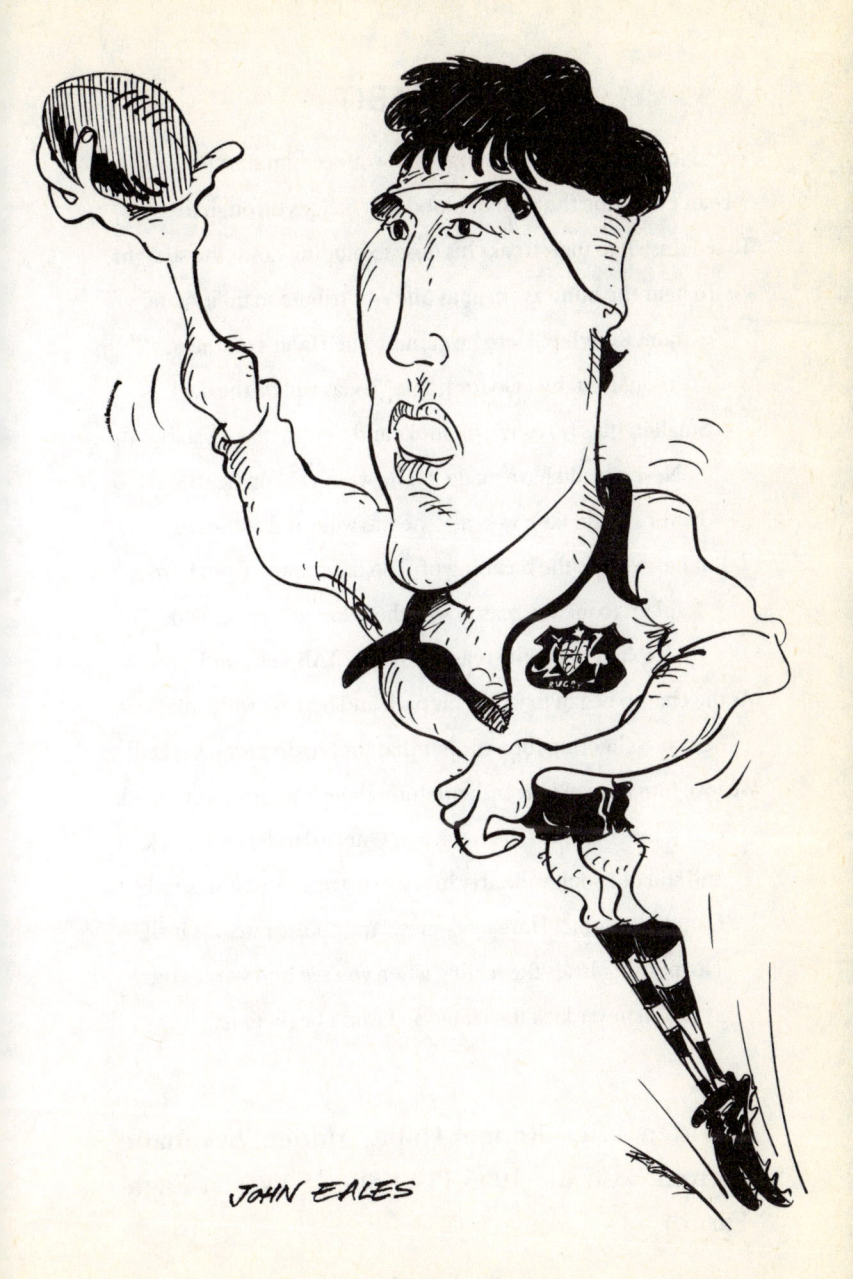

HEROES

JOHN EALES

THE HABIT

Nothing beats the feeling when you see him start to fly,
I can't describe the rush of blood that echoes through the sky.
To see the white that streaks his nose exploding down the straight,
To hear the punters cheer as one — a tribute to their mate:
'C'mon, Roughie! Here he comes! The Habit's on the way!
C'mon, Roughie! Go for home! Today will be the day!'
Small in stature, rough on looks and slow to make a start,
Never would have made it if he wasn't big on heart.
Never should have won it — he was wide and at the rear,
But never knew the meaning of 'Too hard to win from here'.
Explain to me the reason why the other jockeys smiled.
Explain to me the reason why the TAB went wild.
As the champ began to weave his path and Scrivo's whip attacked,
They were cheering for a runner that they hadn't even backed!
We love him here in Queensland, though he hails from Kiwi stock.
Throw his colours in the book and Queenslanders will flock.
And still our souls will carry him when greener pastures call:
'C'mon, Roughie! Here he comes!' Your pulse rate says it all.
No, nothing beats the feeling when you see him start to fly,
I'll never kick the Habit, so I won't begin to try.

(Written after Rough Habit, ridden by Shane Scriven, won the 1995 PJ O'Shea Stakes at Eagle Farm.)

THE PRETTY BAT OF WAUGH

His team mates call him Affie, the forgotten Waugh they say,
But no one will forget the ton he rattled up today.
Now I don't subscribe to panic, but my heart was numb with shock,
When the Kiwis had the neck of Aussie cricket on the block.
The axe was poised to plummet like it did in '92,
Enter 'The Assassin' and the job he had to do.
He blessed his sacred battle pad, he wrapped it 'round his thigh,
He saw another stickman in the corner of his eye.
To every roaring corner, the attack was soon dispatched,
He focused on that stickman, then in triumph it was scratched.
Limb by limb he scratched it, he was knackered for the score,
And the game was made Australia's in the name of Affie Waugh.

His team mates call him Junior 'cos he came out after Tugga,
And like his older brother, he's a bloody handy bugger.
Whether brandishing a lump of wood or sending down the seed,
When he cuts the opposition up, he really makes them bleed,
And when the edge of error sends a scud to second slip,
He's the man you want behind it with the glue that smears his grip.
Never one to sell the drama in the face of brilliant skill,
He makes the game look easy — if it's there to catch, he will,
And when you think you've seen it all, he'll show you something more,
Then you'll shake your head and whisper, 'You're a legend
Junior Waugh!'

His team mates call him Pretty, and I s'pose they prob'ly should,
'Cos all that I can say is that he's pretty bloody good.
There is genius in his chromosomes and cricket in his claret,
He can read a situation like a gypsy reading tarot,
And in my opinion something else that puts him out in front,
Is his reading of the form guide and his prowess on the punt.
In the middle, he'll be murdering the leather with a thirst,
In the drinks break, he'll be kicking home the favourite in the first.
And that's the way he plays the game, the risk is worth the glory,
If he fails, he'll get 'em next time; if he fires, end of story.
It is then that you'll be treated, you'll be looking on in awe,
And you'll wish you had *your* fifty on the pretty bat of Waugh.

(Written after Mark Waugh's gutsy century in Australia's World Cup quarter final victory over New Zealand in 1996.)

HEROES

MARK WAUGH

LLL (LEAPIN' LEROY LOGGINS)

They could paint the Story Bridge bright pink,
And traffic still would flow.
The big town clock could miss a chime,
And people wouldn't know.
If they changed the name of Queen Street Mall,
The shoppers still would come.
If the Brekky Creek ran out of beer,
The boys would switch to rum.
But Leroy, mate, I'll tell ya straight,
It just won't be the same
When your number 30 singlet
Has been taken from the game.
For fifteen years, those skinny pins
Have sizzled down our courts,
Making basketball at Boondall
One of Brisbane's favourite sports.
As a Bullet 'Leroy Loggins'
Is the perfect definition —
So fast to blast a team away
With deadly ammunition,
With rebounds, slams and monster jams,
With defence tightly stickin',
The way he walks, the way he talks —
'Well, choke ma sister's chicken!'

Heroes

LEROY LOGGINS

He's the coolest cat I've ever seen,

And that includes the Fonz.

Players come in singlets,

Only legends come in bronze.

If they blew up Moreton Island,

Well, I s'pose I'd go to Straddie,

But the day that leapin' Leroy quits

Is gonna be a saddy.

(Written during Leroy Loggins' testimonial year in 1996.)

YOU LITTLE BLOODY RIPPER

The German keeper waited — she was very highly rated,
Though she looked a little frightened all the same,
For she was staring down the barrel at the flying Ripper Farrell —
'Twas a sight to scare the bravest in the game.

As the keeper caught her eye, then she knew the reason why,
And she also knew the feeling of 'too late',
'Cos with born determination that would turn to jubilation,
Hockey's chocolate lover struck a winning fate.

To the final even keener, where we wiped out Argentina,
And the excellence of Farrell didn't stop.
On a day she won't forget, every challenge faced was met,
And this Townsville girl was standing at the top.

Yes — her future has been mapped and the folks 'round here are rapt.
She is treasured more than Cinderella's slipper,
And from sidelines on the field, in a tone most often squealed,
You will hear them shout, 'You little bloody ripper!'

(Written after the hockey World Cup in 1995.)

GARY ABLETT

The Eleventh Commandment

The holy book supposes

That a bearded cat named Moses

Put his heavy duty hikers on and dragged 'em through the sand,

As he headed up a mission

With a team in good condition,

And a burning apparition of a far-off promised land.

And indeed the heads were turning,

When the sacred bush was burning,

prompting Moses, on his team's request, to go and check it out.

And the smoke, it choked his airway,

As a hand from heaven's stairway

Punched a likely pair of tablets with a God almighty clout,

And the guru being gifted,

Caught the tablets, which he lifted,

Then announced them as commandments from the corridors of heaven.

Only ten had been expected,

So he stood to be corrected,

When he took the stage and told them that, in fact, there were eleven.

'There cannot be eleven!'

Cried the Hebrew wearing 7,

'What does this bloke take us for — a pack of bloody fools!'

But the jeering turned to cheering,

For the words that they were hearing —

The eleventh read as follows: 'Thou shall play Australian Rules.'

And the moment must have figured —

Moses' kicking boot was triggered,

For he spiral-punted one above a host of screaming packs.

And the mark that he was feeding,

For a million Christians leading,

Could have ended in disaster as they climbed each other's backs.

But the saviour wouldn't cop it,

Fearing most, that they would drop it,

So he called on every skill he had and all the games he'd played.

And he wasn't just a dreamer —

No — he flew to take a screamer,

And because he was the ump as well, the mark was duly paid.

Heroes

It was really quite amazing,

And the people stood there gazing

Up towards the great Messiah who had marked the holy tablet.

And I think that they were knowing,

When the number 5 was showing

On a blue-and-white striped singlet, and the angels chanted 'Ablett'.

Now you prob'ly thinked I've jipped yas,

But the truth is in the scriptures,

So I bid you have a read of them before you call me odd.

But if your Bible's somehow skinnier,

Then I'd go out to Kardinia,

Where still, these days, the crowds give praise to number 5 — their God.

(Written after watching Gary Ablett take another screamer in season 1996.)

Plugger (Ballad of the Beast)

On this great big lump of granite

That we like to call our planet

There are mysteries and monsters that intrigue us with suspicion

And of those that often feature

There's that ugly Loch Ness creature

Big Foot, werewolves, aliens and certain politicians

But the latest breed of myst'ry

That will take its place in hist'ry

Is a singlet-wearing, fullback-scaring, giant-booted slugger

A half-man, half-Swan mutation

With a fearsome reputation

That the scientists of AFL have come to label Plugger

He's as wide as Sydney Harbour

He's as mean as Don King's barber

He's as tough as Dirty Harry, he's as strong as Noah's Ark

And to see all that combining

Is a concept worth defining

In a goal square full of traffic it will often equal 'mark'

HEROES

Yes there's been some sightings lately
That have pleasured Swans fans greatly
None so highly praised as when he kicked his 100th goal

And if the red and white tight-shorters
Have the heart of their supporters
Then I reckon it is fair to say that Plugger has their soul

So if the X-Files want a story
And a taste of Sydney's glory
Then I think that they should monitor the sacred SCG

For around the forward pocket
They will find a beast called Lockett
And the beast in all its glory is a mighty sight to see

But they shouldn't try and chain him
Or in any way restrain him
For that bicepted lump of seasoned rump can steamroll any bugger

Then when he's shouldered, marked and kicked 'em
They'll be just another victim
In another grave that bears the sentence — 'Taken out by Plugger'.

The Great Goldrush (Part II)

The 26th Olympic Games have glued me to my chair

and my ears are now infected with 'Advance Australia Fair'

For every time that anthem pumps a chorus through my heart

Another dream is written and the backbone shivers start

Ah, the guts of Kieren Perkins — what a freak that young bloke is!

And super Suzie in the butterfly — she'll bring it back to Briz!

There was Freeman on the running track with hunger in her eye

And a host of other Aussies with an appetite to fly

That McPaul can hoik a javelin and Stefan's bronze was cool

Diamond's golden bullet nearly knocked me off ma' stool!

Gary Neiwand tried his heart out, Robbie Peden's no pedestrian

The Awesome Foursome kicked some arse and so did our equestrian!

Michael Murphy's doing somersaults, our hockey teams are set

The Opals and the Boomers and the Woodies at the net

And I thought the Games were over but the bravest tales weren't told

Because our Para-Olympians showed the world they too were made of gold

Ya know I'd love to mention everyone but time does not permit
You could get a mile of paper and the names might still not fit
They're the names that stand rewarded for their courage and devotion
And when that flag is flying, it will challenge their emotion
Look into the athlete's eye, I bet you'll find a tear
And you might cry one with them, it's a pride you shouldn't fear
Because it's times like this our wide brown land is just the perfect possie
And it's times like this it's bloody great, it's great to be an Aussie.

But like those dreams where you're flying through the sky without a worry in the world, only to discover that your arms aren't really wings, before falling to a waking scream, so too this dream turned into a nightmare.

The heroes he had been cheering from his nocturnal grandstand suddenly disappeared. The sky grew dark and with thunder rumbling on the horizon, he saw himself standing alone on a great red stage. It looked to him very much like a huge rock in the middle of nowhere and there he was, frightened and confused, reciting these words to endless kilometres of nothing:

> *. . . Places, faces, Guinness chasers, racing through his mind,*
> *Have you ever had the feeling that you've left something behind?*
> *For even as he reached the end, he started reminiscing,*
> *If only he could find the part that all along was missing.*
> *Every night he tossed and turned in dreams of something lost,*
> *In a world of hidden secrets, he would search at any cost.*
> *He'd come so far to find it — now he faced his greatest fear,*
> *The hardest thing of all was that it seemed so very near . . .*

He woke in a sweat of terror. Pins and needles shot down his spine and every hair on his body was standing on end. The rash was everywhere and with the lump in his throat, he couldn't even scream. Unable to move for a few seconds, he sat alone on the edge of his bed, gathering his thoughts. This was getting out of hand.

By the time he had showered and rugged up for a trip to the doctor, the symptoms had vanished, but he made the trip anyway. The doctor's diagnosis didn't surprise him all that much: 'You're as fit as fiddle, son. Absolutely nothing wrong with you.'

He was a little relieved at that, although he had already made up his mind about one thing — he'd be straight in to see his local GP, Doctor Nash, when he got back to Australia in a week's time.

Chapter Eleven

Judgement Day

JUDGEMENT DAY

He had that same lonely rock recital nightmare every night for the next week, until destiny *did* become something real, and fate *did* bring him to it.

It was somewhere on a runway that the missing piece was found.
He knew that as the tyre rubber touched Australian ground,
That 'something' he was searching for was with him from the start.
Every day he spent away, it never left his heart.
He would not forget the beauty and adventure that he met,
But of all the vivid memories, there's one I won't forget.
The great romance of travel took a young bloke by the hand,
To the place that he was missing — to his home — the lucky land.

Sometimes you have to go a long way to appreciate how good you've got it and how lucky you are to be living in a land where lawyers get the opportunity to become poets.

There was still one more thing for me to do.

GREEN AND GOLD MALARIA

The day would soon arrive when I could not ignore the rash.
I was obviously ill and so I called on Doctor Nash.
This standard consultation would adjudicate my fate.
I walked into his surgery and gave it to him straight:
'Doc, I wonder if you might explain this allergy of mine,
I get these pins and needles running up and down my spine.
From there, across my body, it will suddenly extend —
My neck will feel a shiver and the hairs will stand on end.
And then there is the symptom that a man can only fear —
A choking in the throat, and the crying of a tear.'
Well, the Doctor scratched his melon with a rather worried look.
His furrowed brow suggested that the news to come was crook.
'What is it, Doc?' I motioned. 'Have I got a rare disease?
I'm man enough to cop it sweet, so give it to me, please.'
'I'm not too sure,' he answered, in a puzzled kind of way.
'You've got some kind of fever, but it's hard for me to say.
When is it that you feel this most peculiar condition?'
I thought for just a moment, then I gave him my position:
'I get it when I'm standing in an Anzac Day parade,
And I get it when the anthem of our native land is played,
And I get it when Meninga makes a Kiwi-crunching run,
And when Border grits his teeth to score a really gutsy ton.

JUDGEMENT DAY

THE GREAT AUSSIE MOSSIE
CARRIER OF GREEN & GOLD MALARIA

I got it back in '91 when Farr-Jones held the Cup,
And I got it when Japan was stormed by Better Loosen Up.
I get it when the Banjo takes me down the Snowy River,
And Matilda sends me waltzing with a billy-boiling shiver.
It hit me hard when Sydney was awarded with the Games,
And I get it when I see our farmers fighting for their names.
It flattened me when Bertrand raised the boxing kangaroo,
And when Perkins smashed the record, well, the rashes were true blue.
So tell me, Doc,' I questioned. 'Am I really gonna die?'
He broke into a smile before he looked me in the eye.
As he fumbled with his stethoscope and pushed it out of reach,
He wiped away a tear and then he gave this stirring speech:
'From the beaches here in Queensland to the sweeping shores of Broome,
On the Harbour banks of Sydney where the waratah's in bloom.
From Uluru at sunset to the mighty Tasman Sea,
In the Adelaide cathedrals, at the roaring MCG.
From the Great Australian Bight up to the Gulf of Carpentaria,
The medical profession call it "green and gold malaria".
But forget about the text books, son, the truth I shouldn't hide.
The rash that you've contracted here is "good old Aussie pride".
I'm afraid that you were born with it and one thing is for sure —
You'll die with it, young man, because there isn't any cure.'

THE LUCKY LAND

The great romance of travel took a young bloke by the hand,
To the dream of something better in an unknown foreign land
The winds of autumn whispered for his spirit to belong
With an atmosphere he tasted in the lyrics of a song.
He packed his bag, he packed his flag, an old guitar as well.
The road would write the story that he knew he had to tell.
He counted down the days and still that song was on his brain,
Until the customs desk at Brisbane sent him out to meet his plane.
At last his soul was flying from a town of obligations
At the point of no return . . . and he had no reservations.
The truth was out there somewhere — deep inside he knew it,
And if destiny was something real, then fate would bring him to it . . .

He knew the night was London when the stars above him snowed,
and he walked the famous crossing on the tar of Abbey Road.
He touched the block that chilled the flesh of many royal necks,
felt a dose of Ashes history that a tour of Lords injects.
He sang the song of Cardiff, 'Bread of Heaven, Wales Forever',
At Lansdowne Road he belted out a verse of 'Nae, No, Never'.
Dublin turned to publin in the days that followed that,
On bar room stools from Tommy Wrights to Scruffy Murphs, he sat.
He sailed the ring of Kerry and he scaled the Cliffs of Moher,
He drank the brown in Galway town and toasted to the pour.

He kissed the stone at Blarney and he saw Killarney's splendour,
Then he marched the streets of Belfast reading signs of 'no surrender'.
On a cold Croaghpatrick Mountain peak, he stood in awesome solace,
He smiled at Stirling Castle in the name of William Wallace.
He danced upon the woodwork where The Beatles once rehearsed,
Then he heard the roar at Aintree as the horses jumped the first.
... Places, faces, Guinness chasers, racing through his mind,
Have you ever had the feeling that you've left something behind?
For even as he reached the end, he started reminiscing,
If only he could find the part that all along was missing.
Every night he tossed and turned in dreams of something lost,
In a world of hidden secrets, he would search at any cost.
He'd come so far to find it — now he faced his greatest fear,
The hardest thing of all was that it seemed so very near ...

It was somewhere on a runway that the missing piece was found,
He knew that as the tyre rubber touched Australian ground.
That 'something' he was searching for was with him from the start,
Every day he spent away, it never left his heart.
He would not forget the beauty and adventure that he met,
But of all the vivid memories, there's one I won't forget.
The great romance of travel took a young bloke by the hand,
To the place that he was missing — to his home — the lucky land.

What's Mazda doing in Rupert McCall's Sports Poetry Book?

It's no coincidence
It's no surprise at all
That Mazda has an ad
In this book by R. McCall
Coz just like rhyming Rupert
We also love our sport
And if you're a tad cynical
Just look at our support
Of sweaty athletes everywhere
In every sport that's going
(Except, of course, mud wrestling
And, of course, dwarf throwing)
We help out those in cricket
And those in rugby games
We give to souls who like lawn bowls
So let us name some names
We can talk about Vic Wilson
We can talk about Mike Klim
(We can't talk about Dave Wansbrough
Coz nothing rhymes with him)
I guess this all just proves
What generous folks we are
We hope that you remember this
Next time you buy a car

mazda

MAZ 3153